FOOD BLOGGING 101

By
Malika Harricharan Bowling

FOOD BLOGGING 101
By Malika Harricharan Bowling

ACKNOWLEDGMENT

My sincere appreciation for all the food bloggers and all the others who helped make this book possible.

And for the special interviews in this book, I an grateful to:
*Keren Brown – Author, **Food Lovers' Guide to Seattle***
*Sucheta Rawal – Founder, Non-profit, **GO Eat Give***
*Dennis Byron (aka Ale Sharpton), **Beer Blogger, Speaker and Event Host***

OTHER BOOKS and WEBSITES
By Malika Harricharan Bowling

Food Lovers' Guide to Atlanta: The Best Restaurants, Markets & Local Culinary Offerings (Food Lovers' Series)

https://www.facebook.com/AssociationofFoodBloggers

http://atlanta-restaurantblog.com

Table of Contents

Introduction

According to a recent search of Technorati, it appears that there are over 20,000 food blogs in existence as this book is being written. That number will only continue to climb as more enter the blogging world. That may sound somewhat daunting if you are now considering your journey into the blogosphere, but now is a great time to get into food blogging as there are so many avenues that you can use to gain traction.

For the purposes of this book, I'm going to assume that you are dedicated to building your blog, readership and perhaps interested in making a living from your blog. Otherwise, you wouldn't have purchased this product, would you? If you don't have the time to devote to building your blog and your brand, then it is in your best interest to wait until you do to begin the process.

So, why did I write this book? A couple reasons. I really dislike how companies have stopped caring about their employees. There's no loyalty or respect in most companies anymore. I'd like people to know how easy it is to start your own business, with blogging. Of course, it requires hard work and dedication, but it is so worth it to do something you love. Giving others the skills to begin blogging is one way I can help people break free from being slaves to jobs they despise.

Also, I have been asked by others for advice on how to start a blog: Where to begin? How to find their voice, and how to gain readers? I wanted to share the knowledge I have gained in my years of writing, blogging and Social Media consulting with others who are as passionate about food as I am.

Chapter 1 – Setting Up Your Blog

For the purposes of this book, I'll only be discussing setting up your blog in Wordpress and plugins and other items associated with that. I know there are other content management systems for blogs, but Wordpress is the most user-friendly and the only one that truly allows you to own your domain name outright. Even if you choose to use another platform, you will still benefit from 90 percent of everything discussed in this book.

If you have a blog that is currently hosted on a system other than Wordpress, it is rather simple to transfer it to Wordpress with a couple steps. That is the beauty of all blogs – content is separate from design. Your host can help you with transferring your blog from another CMS to Wordpress.

Wordpress has two different types of systems. Hosted and self-hosted. A hosted site on the Wordpress platform will look like this: YourDomain.wordpress.com. When you own your own domain it will simply look like YourDomain.com.

You'll want to own your Domain for a couple reasons. One being it looks much more professional to own your domain versus having it on a hosted site. Also, you truly don't "own" your site name if it is hosted on Wordpress' domain or another site such as Blogspot.

Setting up my blog on Wordpress

First you will need to register a domain name. You can do this at any place like Go Daddy or Online-Domain-Names.com. It should cost approximately $10 to do this. Registering a domain name is a yearly thing. Make sure to renew (your domain registrant will usually send out a reminder email close to your renewal date) otherwise you could lose your domain name ownership.

Once you are done with registering a domain name, you need to find hosting. Hosting is where the files on the site "live." Hosting is sometimes paid on a monthly basis but usually on a yearly basis as well. Expect to pay about $5 to $10 per month for hosting. One of the good things about most companies like Hostgator, for example is that you can host unlimited numbers of sites with one plan. So, you could have 100 or more blogs if you like!

Once you sign up for hosting you will be given a login to your C-panel where just about everything you would need access to is located. You will also be given Nameservers. This is where any blog you have registered will point to. So, once you get these nameservers, you'll need to log back into wherever you registered your domain and enter these nameservers.

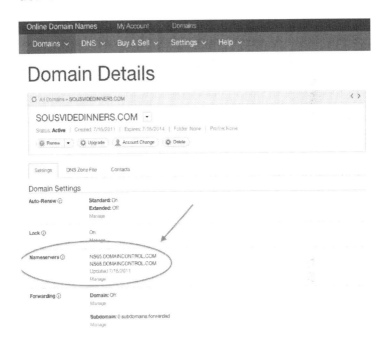

It may take about an hour for the change to occur but it is usually within about five or ten minutes. Once this is done, you will need to add your domain name to your hosting account. Then you will go back into your Cpanel and install Wordpress. Scroll down to something that says Mojo Market or you may even see the Wordpress logo as below and click on it. This should give Wordpress as an option. Don't fret if this seems too complicated. Any good hosting company should have a number to call where they can walk you through these steps.

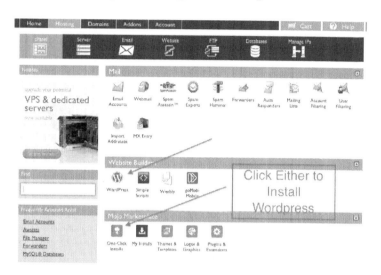

Choose Wordpress and click on install a fresh new version.

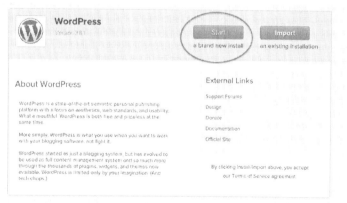

From there after you click on Wordpress, you'll be given the list of domains that are hosted with this company and with one click you can install Wordpress. You'll then be given a link, user id and password to login to your fresh Wordpress installation.

If all this a bit too technical for you, then hire someone to do it for you. While it is fantastic to know how to do everything related to your blog, there are some things that just aren't necessary. Your skill is the content creator, not the technical person. Always remember that.

Most web professionals will charge about $50 to install Wordpress on your site. However, there is a site called Fiverr.com where individuals will do tasks like these for only five dollars.

So, where do you find someone if you don't feel comfortable using a site like Fiverr.com? I'd recommend by asking around. Ask your facebook friends who they recommend for web services. If that fails go to odesk.com, elance.com or guru.com and you will be able to find someone who can do this for you. Once you get Wordpress installed it is pretty much plug and play.

Whatever you choose to do, please don't get bogged down on this initial setup. It is a one time thing and something that can be frustrating if you have never done anything like it before. I want you to succeed and become a successful blogger. There is nothing wrong with outsourcing.

I am not a technical person, and I outsource everything I can, because my time is better spent creating books and courses that teach others how to be successful bloggers. Your time is better spent creating exceptional content for your blog, networking in the blogging community and testing the methods that will help you to monetize your blog.

Choosing A Name for Your Blog and Basic Setup

This is really important and obviously something you should put a lot of thought into. Pick a name that reflects you and your style. I made the mistake of choosing my blog name solely based on search engine optimization. My name, Atlanta Restaurant Blog, has severed me well as far as coming up in search terms, but had I had to choose another name, I would choose something without the world "blog" in it.

While this might sound a little contrary to what we are talking about, try to think of your blog as not a blog at all but an online magazine. It is a small thing, but there is a different connotation that comes with an online magazine vs. a blog. An online magazine brings with it much more credibility. Think of sites like Eater, Urbanspoon, Urban Daddy and the like. All of these are essentially blogs, but because of they aren't characterized as such, they have much more credibility. Heck, even the New York Times is hosted on Wordpress.

Here are some more tips for naming your blog:
Make sure it is original and not similar to someone else's blog name.
URL: Get the .com or .net if possible. .me, .co, or .us are just too obscure
Keep it short. If it is too long it will be hard to remember and could even hurt SEO.

Bear in mind, once you start to get some traction for your blog, it will be very difficult to change the name. People will get to know you and your blog as that name. And more importantly, other sites may start to link to individual posts on your blog. I have a post that is linked to from the Huffington Post. If I were to change the name of my blog, there's no way I'd be able to reach anyone there to update the link. It would be lost forever. We'll discuss later on why these inbound links are important.

Choosing your Theme

Snapshot of the term "wordpress theme" when typed in Google

If you aren't aware, there are hundreds of thousands of Wordpress themes out there. Don't be like so many others and get caught up in the minutia of choosing a design. Your very first priority should be content more than anything else. That is what is going to bring your traffic and gain readership.

Now, I'm not saying stick to the default theme and not worry about the design. Make it look decent, but don't be so tied to the design that you don't find time to write. My blog took several iterations before it came to the design I am using now. And remember, you can always change the theme of your blog because the content is separate from the design.

Uploading your theme

Once you choose the theme you have to upload it from the Admin /Appearances section of your blog. Make sure to activate it after you upload it.

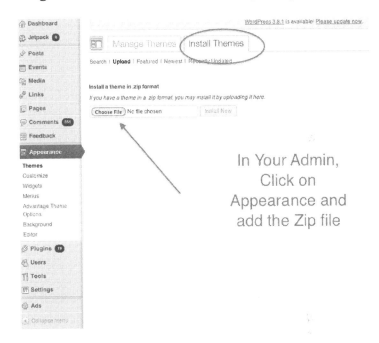

As far as themes, I'll tell you right from the beginning I've never paid for a theme. I've always used the free ones. That is what I recommend anyone starting out should do. If you aren't making money from the blog, then don't buy a theme.

That being said, themes that you do buy don't cost that much – between $40 and $70 each. The benefit of buying a theme is that there is customer support on how to integrate it with your ideal design and also it should be more easy to use and navigate than a free theme. If you do choose to purchase a theme and have difficulty using it and there isn't much support, ask for a refund and just install a free them for the time being.

Some resources for themes:

Wordpress: Wordpress.org/extend/ themes
StudioPress: ww.studiopress Paid
Theme Forest: Paid themes

Expert Blogger

Have you heard of Darren Rowse? He started Problogger which has led to much success for him. He originally started a photography blog which garnered 15,000 views per day. He became one of the first six figure bloggers ever.

Newsletter signup

You may want to consider adding an email newsletter to your blog as well. This is a terrific element that I don't see many bloggers doing. For now, use Mailchimp. It is free for up to 500 subscribers. Once you get over that number you can evaluate if you want to continue with them or use a paid service such as Constant Contact. However, I use Mailchimp and find it to be very user friendly.

It costs nothing to implement an email signup form. Once you sign up you'll be given a snippet of HTML code to add to your blog. You can add this in a text block of one of your sidebar widgets (we'll go over widgets in a later chapter). Even if you aren't ready to send out a newsletter for a couple months, at least put the signup form on your blog so you can start collecting email addresses.

This could be very powerful later on. Having a large email list is great for selling products. And if this seems daunting – coming up with terrific content for your blog plus sending out a weekly or monthly newsletter, don't worry about it. Remember you can get lots of content from restaurant newsletters that you will sign up for.

And once you get a steady form of posts on your site, you can reuse some of them in your newsletters. Don't worry about reusing content. Most readers will never notice it's the same content from your website in your newsletters as long as you continue to provide good articles. So, sending out some of the same articles on a couple newsletters won't hurt anything.

Social Proof

We'll get to the chapter on Social Media profiles and getting those all setup in a later chapter.

However, I want you to incorporate a couple of items into your site when you are working on getting it setup along with social media images.

The first thing is to encourage your readers to sign up for your RSS feed. When readers sign up for your RSS feed they can be delivered your content to their email inbox when it is published. That way, you can have readers coming back to your site without having to lure them back time and time again. Also, when you have an RSS feed you can display how many readers have signed up. Don't do this until you have at least 100 subscribers. People have a herd mentality. If you show that a lot of people aren't following your blog (yet) they will be less likely to want to subscribe themselves.

Feedburner and Feedblitz are two options to allow readers to sign up with their email addresses and get content delivered right into their inbox whenever a new post goes live. This way they don't have to keep checking back with your blog to see if you've posted new content.

All of these elements including your social media sharing buttons like Facebook, Twitter, Pinterest, Instagram, etc should all be "above the fold," which is the area of your blog that can be seen without having to scroll down.

Plugins

You know how with smart phones there are a ton of apps to do whatever you want? Well, plugins are like apps for Wordpress. Want to add a calendar function? Want to automatically share updates to Facebook? Easily incorporate ads to your blog? Whatever you want to do, there's a plugin for that. Plugins can easily be found by searching within your admin dashboard on Wordpress. Be wary of plugins that don't have lots of reviews and never install a plugin that someone has emailed or asked you to download.

You can easily add plugins in the same way you add themes.

SEO Title Tag plugin – This plugin as it states helps with being found in the search engines.

Search Meter Plugin – This plugin displays what the popular searches were on your blog, but it also shows the unsuccessful searches on your blog, or what visitors searched for but didn't find. This is helplful because if you have a topic or restaurant that is what your readers are looking for, it will clue you in.

Social sharing plugins—

Share This –
http://wordpress.org/extend/plugins/share-this/
This plugin will add a small link to your theme, and a popup with the different icons that will open once the user clicks on the link.

Sociable – http://push.cx/sociable
This plugin will add the icons of the selected social sites directly into your template.

Tagging

Every time you enter a post there is a box to add what are called "tags." These identify and categorize your posts. Make sure to tag items properly. Tagging is a huge help in being found by the search engines. Two to five tags per article is a good number. Any more and you may get penalized by the search engines for stuffing keywords. In the beginning you may not see how beneficial tagging is but as your blog is around for several months, tagging will become more valuable.

Over time as you start to see an increase in search traffic you will begin to notice things like your internal tags helping you rank better for secondary keyword phrases and how important the title of your blog article is.

Pages you should add to your blog

About Me

You may already have an "About Me" page on your site, but if it's something you've put up rather quickly without much effort into it, go back and revisit it. Instead of talking about your site being so amazing, talk about the benefit readers will get from it. Your main goal is to use this as a tool to establish a relationship with your readers.

Really put some thought into your "about me" page. Share your personal story with your readers. How did you get into food writing? Why are you so passionate about it? Your "about me" page is the only way to develop a rapport with your readers in the beginning and to really connect with them. Share as much personal information about yourself that you feel comfortable with.

Share your life story. On my About Me page, I talk about my mom dying when I was young and the fact that my father wasn't a good cook, which led me and my brother to becoming huge foodies. Aim for your story to be at least 1000 words. Keep it on focus though. Relate it to food writing, how you got started and what is unique about you and your blog.

When it comes to food blogging many food bloggers want to keep their identity a secret. As it goes with most food critics, they do not disclose their identity. But I highly recommend against this. Putting up pictures of yourself is one of the biggest ways to connect with readers. It also is imperative if you want to go to media events. More about this in a later chapter.

List of reviews / recipes

Make your content easy to find. Of course you'll have a search bar on your site as most themes come with that by default, but a listing of reviews or recipes is very helpful to readers as well. Perhaps they don't remember the name of the restaurant they are looking for but if they saw it on a list, they'd be able to pick it out. If you have a recipe blog, maybe you might categorize your recipes into types of food: like appetizer, dessert, salad, etc. Again, I can't say it enough: make your content easy to find.

Contact page

I'm always surprised at the amount of blogs I see that do not have any way to contact them. If you don't want to put an email address out there, there should at least be a contact form. You never know why someone would want to contact you. Maybe they want you to try a product or a food sample. Maybe they want to invite you somewhere for a short trip. You want to be contacted by PR companies for opportunities. You need to have a simple, easy way to be contacted. Use the plugin Contact Form 7 from Wordpress.

It is super easy to setup. Download and install the plugin. The plugin itself then gives you what is called a short code which looks something like this [contact form]. That's all you need to add a contact form to your site. Then simply make sure to put the email address you want in the form.

Advertising / Sponsor Page

You will need to spend quite a bit of time creating content before you are approached by advertisers. Traffic is the bottom line to getting advertising. However, you should always have a page listing that advertising is available, otherwise known as a media kit. It looks professional and you can be qualified by PR professionals, etc. if you have a page that shows all your traffic statistics.

What do these terms mean?

Unique Visitors: These are the number of people individually who have visited your website. If you have a loyal friend who visits 20 times a month they will only be counted once.

Pageviews: How many web pages display. This is usually measured in a given amount of time like a month.

See a sample below of relevant statistics. You can find these by visiting Alexa.com.

As of September 2013:
Unique visitors: 21,000 +
Page Views: 185,000 +
US Rank: 301,223
Global Rank: 1,002,588

Sample content for ad page:

Payment
All prices below are in USD. Payment is via PayPal.com. You can use your PayPal balance, your credit card or your bank account. Please email me at email@yourdomain.com with the package you are interested in and I will send an invoice via Paypal.

Package 1 – The Text Link Package

Cost: $25 Per Month
What you get: 1 site-wide text link at the top of the   page.
Note: All text links placed on the website have the "no follow" tag applied.

Package 2 – 125 x 125 Prime Box Banner

Cost: $50 Per Month

What you get: Your 125x125 box banner in the top right primary position (see "Advertise Here" blocks)

Benefits: Your campaign is placed on all pages including the homepage, in the right top column prime sponsor area.
You will need to supply your own 125x125 pixel banner. JPEG or GIF are accepted, no animation is permitted and please keep file size low. You may change your banner at any time. Instructions for submitting your banner are below.

Package 3 – 468*60 Prime Box Banner

Cost: $100 Per Month
What you get: Your 468*60 box banner in the bottom center of the website. Benefits: Your campaign is placed on all pages including the homepage, in the bottom center of the page.
You will need to supply your own 468*60 pixel banner. JPEG or GIF are accepted, no animation is permitted and please keep file size low.

You may change your banner at any time. Instructions for submitting your banner are below.

Submit Your Media

After making payment please send through links to your banners (host them on your server), text link anchor text and URL(s) to link to email@yourdomain.com. As your banner images will be hosted on your own site, you can change them any time you wish.

Dissected Blog Post

Posts – This is where you will spend the majority of your time. Click "Add a new post", and you will see a blank canvas similar to the image below. The header is key. Think about names and titles you would type into a search engine to find what you are writing about.

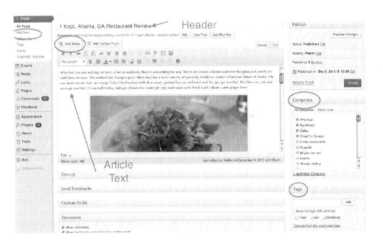

Article text – this is the main body of the post. Here you can add links, bulleted lists, photos and videos. A note about links: the words you use in your links are called anchor text. Make sure they pertain to the link they are describing. Don't use anchor text like "Click Here" or "Buy

Tickets" as these are too vague for search engines. They like to see actual content. Instead use anchor text like "Once again Attack of the Killer Tomato Festival Tickets will sell out quickly" or, "Last month I shared my recipe for Cumin braised lamb shanks."

Tagging and categories – Tags and categories help search engines find your posts too, but they also help users navigate your blog by dividing up your posts by groupings. Categories are groupings that you've set up for your posts to go in. For example you could group recipes by low-fat, vegetarian, or desserts. For reviews I might group them by geographic area, cuisine type or simply "interviews." Tags are unique for each post though you will probably use them over and over again. These tags you type in for each post.

Adding pictures – All pictures you post will most likely be stored on your server (this is with the hosting company.) That is essentially what you are doing when you upload a photo. It is assigned a link and this is where it "lives" on your server. Just click on "Add Media" above the title header. Then upload a picture from your computer.

Resizing images-- Images can be small, medium or large. For the most part, it is best to keep most of your pictures in the large size this will be about 600 pixels wide or slightly more depending on your blog column width. Medium sized images are well if you have lots of pictures to share in a post or want them to be side by side. Choose Align none and medium width to see two pictures side by side.

Got a video to insert or want to insert from YouTube? Go to YouTube and click on the embed code and simply insert it on your blog post. Make sure that you are adding this content with the "text" feature is highlighted and not "visual" otherwise your video won't get embedded.

Chapter 2 -- Goal Setting

When establishing your blog, you need to know what you want from this blog. You may not know exactly what you want to do but you should have a general idea. Perhaps you want to write for a food publication. Maybe you do fantastic photography and are using the blog to showcase your camera skills - perhaps even sell some the pictures you take. Maybe you want to be a recipe consultant or advisor to a restaurant group. There are many reasons why people write blogs. And there are many different areas blog writing can take you.

Exposure

Chronicling your experiences

Build audience / advertising

Getting media invites / complimentary items stuff

If your goal is anything other than simply chronicling your experiences, you'll need to use Social Media to help drive traffic to your blog. Secure you names on Facebook, Twitter, Pinterest and Instagram before launching your blog. You'd be surprised how many people will snatch these names up quickly and hold them for ransom if you don't secure them.

Why is Social Media relevant? Publicists that invite you to events or write about their products want to make sure they are getting the most exposure possible for their clients. While a blog with a high amount of readership is good, it is even better if you post regularly to social media sites and have garnered a following in those as well.

Also, you are in competition with other bloggers for advertising, media invites and free products. Whether you are aware or not, publicists (for the most part) keep active lists of bloggers and their social media sites and followers. It definitely behooves you to have more of a following than your fellow blogger. I know the fact that I have 9,000+ twitter followers helps get me invites to media events and tweet ups.

How Often to Write

The easy and best answer is to do as much writing as you possibly can. Have you ever visited sites like Eater.com? They post six to eight times per day. With continuous new content, they are like a super blog, updating constantly. While it is not feasible for most to post this many times per day, it is recommended to at least post five times per week, Monday through Friday for the first year to two of writing your blog.

Still with me? Yes, that does seem like quite a bit. However, the posts don't have to be that long. A post of between 200 and 400 words is adequate. What I recommend doing, is setting a time each week where you can crank out as many posts as possible. If you can set aside 2 hours, you'd be surprised how much you can get done. But this means no texting, social media browsing or surfing while you are writing. Content creation is a breeze, as you'll see in the Content Creation chapter.

When fleshing out these items keep in mind that as the creator of the blog content creation is only one part of the job of a successful blog. You will need to keep an editorial calendar. You can easily setup a calendar in Google for free. This will help remind you of upcoming holidays. Aren't these mega important to food blogging? It will also give you a glance at what is coming up. You will also need to make time for these roles:

Chief Information Officer: Keep up to date on all technical issues pertaining to your blog. Updates, bugs, backups and all regular maintenance of your blog.

Editor: Edit everything you write to make sure it is accurate, makes, sense, and is free of grammatical errors.

Food Stylist: Before you take that picture of the fabulous lamb chops you've cooked, make sure it is laid out perfectly and free of any extra sauce. In a restaurant you'll have to do your best to photograph entrees showing them in their best appearance.

Marketing and Publicity: Network to get your name out there. Always be promoting your content often times attending meetup groups and media events.

Photographer: Take, edit and manage all photography and sometimes videography for your blog.
Recipe Developer: Test recipes to make sure they taste right and that they can be reproduced by those in their kitchen.

Social Media Manager: You will need to make sure to keep every social media platfom you are on updated with new posts / pictures and find clever ways to share this information.

Writer: Oh yeah – back to the main reason you started the blog to write and share your valuable content.

Chapter 3 -- Find Your Voice

"Finding your voice" is really a dreaded phrase. But it adequately describes an integral component of the blogging process-- finding your own writing style. If you talk to any blogger who has been at it for any length of time, they will most likely tell you, you must have your own writing style.

While it is perfectly fine and acceptable to read other blogs for inspiration and a new take on things, trying to emulate another blogger or critic won't work. People can smell it a mile away when you are trying to be something you are not. Finding your voice is really a two-part experience.

1. Writing in a way and tone that feels comfortable to you and

2. Writing articles that your audience likes, responds to and shares. (this is done through commenting, sharing on social networks, etc).

Some people like to be very formal in their writing. Some try to be comical. Some try to be conversational, like they are sitting down with you and telling you about their experience. You need to find a style that suits you.

My writing has evolved from when I began writing in 2008 to where it is now. The best advice is to write in a way you are comfortable with. I'd advise against mean-spirited attacks on chefs, servers or restaurants in general and the use of profanity as that is a sure-fire way to get yourself black-listed from any professional writing assignments or media invites.

Part of finding your voice involves developing a niche. Instead of writing about broad and general topics, focus on a niche. With so many food blogs around, it is more important than ever to have a unique spin on your blog. A blog should be a resource for a small part of the population. Here's what I mean:

Write about dining on a budget

A combination of date night and kid-friendly restaurants

Focus on dual interests: Fashion and Food
These are just a few examples. To find your best combination, think about what your hobbies and interests are. I cannot stress enough that you need to write about something you feel passionate about. You will put the most effort and find the greatest results when you write about those subjects you love.

Engaging with others

Part of finding your voice, includes developing a relationship with your readers. The development of a relationship with people will lead to greater traffic if the interaction is positive. People will value you and want to share your content.

If you converse in a positive way with your readers, they will want to stay in touch with you. Also known as word of mouth, this is the best marketing tool available. Every single way you communicate with your audience and peers should be pleasant and helpful. This includes emails, comments and all social media channels.

Simply put - if they like you and you provide value, traffic will come.
I know I'm beating a dead horse here, but really strive to have positive communication with every person you come in contact with. You never know who is a good contact to have that you can leverage to meet someone else who can help you (think top bloggers, people who have large email lists, journalists, etc.)

Anonymity

When developing your writing style, there is no doubt that the question of anonymity comes into play. Obviously if you want media invites, you don't care about remaining anonymous. But, if you do want to remain anonymous, it is quite difficult in this digital age. Chances are there are many pictures of you floating around that you aren't aware of.

Do you have a Faceook profile? What pictures of yourself are on there? You'll have to delete all of those and tell your friends not to post pictures of you online. This in itself, can be quite a hassle and unless you have a goal of becoming a food critic at some point, not worth it.

While the idea of anonymity is modeled after food critics, the landscape has changed tremendously. Heck, even some food critics are no longer anonymous. So, don't do it because you feel more noble or better about your writing because you aren't known and shell out your own money for meals. You can still write in a fair and balanced way without being anonymous.

If you've been at it for any length of time, I can almost guarantee you will be envious of your peers and the invites they get. Blogging, when done effectively and with passion, can lead to tremendous opportunities. I strongly suggest you put yourself (and by that, I mean your picture) out there. Some of the opportunities I've gotten because of food blogger have led to meeting chefs like Tyler Florence and Marcus

Samuelsson. I've gotten speaking engagements as well as travel opportunities too.

Chapter 4 – Content Creation

When faced with what seems like a daunting task of creating at least five posts per week, you may feel overwhelmed, but it is actually much easier than you think. I'm going to break it down into six different kinds of posts. While you certainly don't have to follow this regimen, I do believe having different kinds of posts keeps it interesting for your readers and the variety helps you.

Aim for your posts to be 400 – 600 words in length. However, posts that are about events or foodie related news can be shorter like 200- 250 words.

Six Types of Posts

Reviews and Recipes

Reviews and/or recipes will probably be the longest and most involved, intense writing for you. I like to refer to these posts as the "anchor" posts for the week. Generally, I keep to one review post per week. For one, it is expensive to continually dine out often. For another, there are only so many restaurants in a given city. If you review three or four per week, you will run out of restaurants quickly. The same goes for recipe writing. It takes many tries to perfect a recipe. So, aiming for just one a week is plenty.

Start your review with a little background about the restaurant. Answer questions for your readers like:

Does this restaurant have a notable chef? What is his background?

Does it boast a terrific wine or cocktail menu?

Is it in a trendy or upcoming neighborhood?

Is it in a historic building?

Is the menu known for something in particular?

Remember, that while items like these may seem like common knowledge to you, these are why readers will come to your blog. They aren't the ones keeping up to date with the newest restaurants, or at least not as much as you do. So, it is your job to supply them with this information. If you have a conversational tone, give a little background as to why you chose this restaurant.

Start in the natural flow of your dinner. Did you start with cocktails or wine? Explain why you chose what you did. Did you have a conversation with the bartender or your server and get recommendations? What recommendations did they make and why? Keep in mind, you want to take your readers through what you went through. By doing this you steer them away from making the mistakes you make. You want to promote value above all else.

Next, move on to appetizers, again explain a little about the options. Even if you didn't order something, you can mention it and tell why you find it intriguing or say you'll be visiting again to sample this. When giving descriptions about items, explain why it tastes good, such as, "the sweet figs mix well with the salty cheese"

Move onto entrees and rinse and repeat. Remember to mix in your opinion or "your voice" into the comments. This is where your readers will come to like you and feel as if they know you. This is one of the most valuable things you can do. If they like what you are saying and feel like they can trust you, they will come back to your blog time and time again.

Obviously, if you indulged in dessert and it was notable, now is the time to mention it. In a wrap-up mention about the service. Was it outstanding, good, fair or poor? Service is a huge part of the restaurant experience and can make or break the favorability of the restaurant to the patron. If you had a positive experience, don't be shy about telling your readers the server's name, so they can visit and ask for them.

Another thing that will make your review stand out from others is other helpful hints about your experience that you share with your audience. Is parking an issue? Is there some lot that is cheaper than others? Are there certain nights that specials are offered?

What is the cost? Cost is important to nearly every consumer nowadays. You can mention price of dishes when you mention them or do a general recap: appetizers range from $9-$12, entrees are $20- $25, and so on. Everyone appreciates this especially men, who might want to take a date there.

Recipes -- Readers love it when you give a little background about a recipe you are sharing. Is it a family recipe that was passed down to you? Is it something you developed for your children? Picky eater in the family? Give your readers a bit of background story so they can get to know you a bit.

Be as descriptive as you can be. You can't be sure if your reader is a novice or an experienced cook. Write your recipe as if you are writing your recipe for someone who is not an experienced cook.

2. Interviews

Interviews are a terrific way to get readers interested in your blog. Chef driven restaurants are quite the rage now with diners. I hear this quote all the time, "Chefs are the new rock stars." They want to know about the chef's history, childhood influences and generally about them as a person.

Here are some sample questions you can ask in your interviews:

Where did your inspiration to cook come from?

Do you have any cooking traditions or recipes that you share with your children?

What is your favorite kitchen tool?

What food is your guilty pleasure?

What is your favorite food trend right now?

Do you have a garden? Do you buy organic foods?

3. News

Readers are hungry for food community news like those in the questions below:

What's opening?

What's closing?

Which chef has popped up at which restaurant or has opened his own restaurant.

4. Lists

Lists are an exceptional way to get people to read your content. People love reading articles that are organized in this fashion. Top 10...and the possibilities are endless. You could write a top 10 cocktail bars in your city, Top 10 places to get Korean barbecue, etc. If you write a recipe blog, write about your Top 10 favorite kitchen tools, or your top 10 online stores to shop for items.

5. Food Events

Food events range from anything to any kind of food festival, restaurant weeks, special restaurant dinners and more. If you are new to the blogosphere, you can email publicists to get on their email lists. They are more than happy to share their clients' events with you as it is free publicity for them. When I began blogging, I didn't know I could do this.

6. Guest Blogging

It is a fantastic idea to offer to guest post on blogs. Usually they will give you a link back to your blog at the end of the post. Do this on several well-known blogs (if they will have you). Don't be offended if they don't want to write for your blog. The idea is to leverage their traffic to get your name out there.

You may be tempted to be lax on your review, but don't be. You want to make a name for yourself and the best way you can do this is by putting your best foot forward and doing your best in your review.

Remember you are doing this to leverage the bloggers' readers. So, it is imperative you have your best writing on the guest post. Let this blogger have the first run of the article for a couple months. After that you can give it away as an incentive for someone to sign up for your newsletter or even use it as content in your newsletter.

Ways to Get Content

Newsletters

When I started blogging, I simply signed up to as many restaurant newsletters as I could to get content for my blog. The great thing about this is so many restaurants do an abysmal job in marketing and getting out their newsletter. So, it would appear that I had unique content that no one else had. The other thing is that most people won't take the time to sign up and read multiple newsletters.

You can also find "Breaking News" for your blog. Since restaurants do such a bad job of sharing information, you can capitalize on this for your blog. I was signed up for a newsletter where the restaurant announced they were shutting down for a couple days for a name change and to remodel. I was able to "break" the story before any other news outlet or blogger and thus, benefited from the traffic.

Another good idea to follow when breaking a story or covering events going on is to put your own twist into it. For example, when I heard that a very popular restaurant that had closed down, was now going to do catering, I did more then mention it on my blog. Since I had visited in the past and reviewed it, I had many pictures of the food. One of the items that guests love was their Tres Leches cake. I included a picture of it, noting that guests can now order this cake once again.

Private Label Rights (PLR)

Private Label Rights are very popular in the online marketing world. They are articles or short reports that are free for anyone to use. You can find them for whatever subject you wish by simply typing in the letters PLR before the keyword you are looking or.

While I think that PLR content is a good resource for say a newsletter or perhaps a sample report you give away on your blog to get people to sign up for your newsletter, I don't recommend relying on this solely for your blog content.

There are two reasons:
You aren't the only one who has access to this content. That means that many people can and do buy these articles and put them on their sites without changing a word. This duplicated content is not good for your Google Rank as they don't like to see duplicated content all over the internet.

It isn't in your voice or style. Remember you need to write articles in your own style to build a relationship with your readers. Besides not being in your voice, PLR articles are often poorly written and do need some editing before being published.
So, now you must be wondering why did I mention it at all? Well, I do think PLR content is good for inspiration. Perhaps you read and article that has a couple good points. You can put your own spin on it and it will help you with content. But I strongly recommend against just putting it up on your blog as is.

8. Outsourcing

If you really want a blog but don't have the time to write, you can outsource your writing by hiring someone to write the posts for you. Finding writers is not a problem. You can easily hire a freelancer to create original content article for your blog. The problem is the cost. Expect to pay about $20 per article. You can always find experienced freelance writers on sites like Elance, Rentacoder, Guru or Fiverr.

The problem with outsourcing is that your personality won't come through. The articles may be keyword optimized, but without a good personality behind the blog, you won't develop a strong audience.

Chapter 5 – Branding

Branding is incredibly important when it comes to blogging. So what is branding? "Branding is a name, term, sign, symbol or design, or a combination of them intended to identify the goods and/or services of one person or group of people and to differentiate them from those of others."

You may not think of yourself or your blog as a brand, but you still are. You need a unified identity on your blog, and on all your social media platforms. You want to be instantly recognizable by people. Whether you choose to brand your blog with a logo or your photo, it is up to you. But whatever you choose, be consistent throughout all platforms. And remember with every post you publish you are developing your brand to your readers.

Design

You want to make sure the design of your blog fits with what you are writing about. Obviously if you are writing a recipe blog, you don't want the header image to be of the beach. In the beginning, I recommend you choose something simple and clean. Remember, you need to create

content more than anything else. That's what brings people to your blog - not a pretty design.
Consistent Writing Style

When we talk about finding your voice, it means that it is your style or the tone in which you write. This could be from conversations to very formal or somewhere in between. Whatever you pick, stick with it. And pick what comes naturally to you. If you feel like you have to try very hard to write in a tone that isn't naturally yours two things will happen:

1. Readers will smell it a mile away and not feel connected to you or want to read your blog.

2. You will find it more of a chore than a pleasure to write and will quickly become bored with the task of writing a blog. Remember the reason to write is because you like it and it gives you pleasure. If it becomes too much of a stress to write you won't continue it.

Same name on all Social Media profiles

This is kind of tricky if you picked a blog name before all the social media explosion. Nevertheless, you want to try and be as consistent as possible and as close to your blog name as possible. Again this all goes back to being instantly recognizable.

Appropriate Tagline

This is pretty self explanatory. You want to pick a tagline that in short, sums up what your blog is all about. Mine is "Restaurant Reviews and Foodie News."

Publishing Schedule

You'll want to have a consistent publishing schedule for your blog posts. Of course, from time to time you can make exceptions. I recommend 5 posts per week, Monday through Friday. You may also want to stick to a certain type of post on certain days.

If you have a recipe blog you might want to think about #MeatlessMonday posts, Wednesday might be an easy recipe to get through that day. Friday might be a brunch recipe since you are going into the weekend. For review sites – you might want to post about early week deals that are going on. Wednesdays might always be a restaurant review. Fridays you may want to talk about a cool event happening that weekend. All these things set the expectations of the reader.

CTA – Call to Action

A call to action is exactly what it sounds like -- asking your readers to do something. Try some of the following calls to action:

Add a comment

Subscribe to RSS feed
Click on an ad
Click an affiliate link (more on this later)
Subscribe to your email list

Of course, you won't know exactly what works until you try everything. For example, if you just wrote an article about the secret ingredients of the best spaghetti sauce recipes, then do use a call to action that refers directly to the content – somewhat like:

"If you want more great recipes like this, subscribe to my blog"

It might seem obvious, but most people need to be led so give them clear sign-posts for what to do next.

Chapter 6 – Getting Traffic

So you've got your blog setup, got your social media profiles setup and are following your publishing schedule. Now where's all the traffic? Unfortunately, just because you have terrific content doesn't mean that anyone is seeing it. There are a series of things you must do to make sure your content gets in front of those who want to read it.

Search Engines

Google is the largest, but Yahoo and Bing are good sources of traffic, too. I still get the greatest amount of traffic from search engines. You may have heard this term before and aren't quite sure what is means. Simply put, Search Engine Optimization is including pertinent keywords related to your site, article or post that help the search engines identify your site and list it when those words are searched for.

This comes into play when thinking about what you will title your posts and how often you use the search terms in your post. And if you have a Wordpress blog, you already have an advantage. Search engines love blogs because they have

49

regularly updated content. But Wordpress makes it easy the way they set up titling (H1 Header, H2 Header) to help you to be found as well.

So, help the search engines help you be found. In other words, think about things you would type into a search engine to find your post. Titling your post "Super Meal Last Night" will not in any way boost your blog in the search engines. But titling it "Big Al's Steakhouse, Dallas, TX Restaurant Review" sure does narrow down what your post is about.

While your restaurant reviews for the most part should have that sort of titling, don't forget to be playful and come up with fun titles too. Here are some that I've used in the past:

Sometimes a Girl Just Needs a Good Pho

Rosa Mexicano's New Menu is Offal Good

The General Muir: Schmear Tactics
You'll want to make sure you repeat the keywords in your post title several times in the main body of your post, but not too much. This shows search engines that the content is relevant. Try to include it about two times in the first paragraph and at least one time in the last paragraph. Depending how long your post is, one or two times within that as well is good. But don't put it too much otherwise you will be guilty

of "keyword stuffing" (definition below) and the search engines (especially google) penalize you for this.

Comment / Forum posts

I won't mislead you. This is a tedious task but still a worthy one. Find forums related to food or recipes. Seek local ones in your community and post in there. Also find some of the bigger blogs in your community and post in the comments section.

Now, it is important to note you should NEVER EVER post simply that you have a blog and a url for people to go visit. First of all no one is going to click on your link because they don't know you. Second, you will just make people angry.

The etiquette of posting in forums and blogs is that you post something helpful or something that adds to the conversation about the topic, not something that gets people to automatically click on your link. And it may take several posts before someone does. But remember, once you add your comment, it will more than likely be there forever. Pick a popular forum that is within food and begin offering helpful contributions.

So why would you post a comment if you can't post a link to your blog? In forum posts you usually have to have a login and with blog commenting you usually have to login with a name and a web address. This with your name and details is also known as your signature. And after you've posted something helpful, some people may choose to click over to your blog.

With blog commenting all you really need to do is focus on two main things:
1)Focus on a couple popular blogs and hone in on them with your commenting.
2)When you comment on these blogs, leave good information like an opposing view or a link to relevant resources. Keep repeating this process on all the blogs on your Blogroll (4 – 5), and you will get the attention of the blogger. This is the beginning of developing a relationship with them.

Links

One of the ways, sites are ranked by Google are the number and quality of links they have coming to them. We just talked about forum and comment postings. This is why it is good that the posts are usually there forever. They are links back to your blog.

Incoming links to your blog are like a "thumbs up" for you blog. The more you have the better. The more important search engines deem the site linking to you, the better for you as well.

Besides forums and comments how else can you get links into your blog?

Social Media Posts –- Make sure to always promote your posts on social media with the appropriate tags for a restaurant so they know you mentioned them. If another blogger has a good article tweet it! It is a great way to get social currency – a nod from another blogger and they are more likely to promote your stuff in the future.

Article Marketing –- Use this method with caution. There are lots of sites like Ezine Articles or any number of places that offer users the chance to upload their own articles for exposure. You have to remember to only write original content. If you try to upload something (like private label rights content) that is readily available online they will know and not publish you.

Some say that if you can upload about 100 articles to Ezine articles you will see some traffic. If you have a specialized blog type (like a type of cuisine, or vegetarian reviews) you might not want to follow this method as the site is saturated with articles.

It is a great way to get traffic if you are willing to put the effort in. And you can really see some results quickly. I highly recommend articles if you are trying to build your brand and you, the writer, as the website.

Don't think that all that original content is only for the other website. Remember you had added an email newsletter to you blog? Well here is where you can use all that great content you put into your Ezine articles.

Blog Roll – Get on other bloggers blog roll. This comes from posting good, relevant content. Also put them on your blog roll too.

Authority sites like Urbanspoon, Yelp and Eater –- Make sure to put the Urbanspoon badge on your blog after a post goes live. This will get traffic to your site from Urbanspoon when people see it while researching the restaurant on US. Urbanspoon has also recently given bloggers more of a spotlight on their review section.

Always put links back to your blog on Yelp if you put a clip of your review there. Change it up a bit. You don't want duplicate content from your blog

Be controversial! Put your own heated opinion about a current event or an important aspect going on in your industry. Be ready to take some heat for your opinion (you may strike a nerve which is a good thing)! Don't argue for the sake of arguing but be prepared to support your opinion.

EXTRA TIP – DIGG

Go to the DIGG home page. When a topic comes up that is very relevant to your blog, leave a comment. Try this as often as you can. You'll see some decent traffic resulting from this.

Your own blog

That's right! Search engines don't penalize you from linking within your blog. There are probably many posts that require a link to a previous post because they compliment each other. Make sure to always link to a previous post if mentioning it by name. If you are talking about a new restaurant that has terrific ceviche – make mention of the previous restaurants you've visited in the past that serve ceviche and link to those posts.

That's a lot to cover. You don't have to do everything at once, but I do want you to see all the ways there are to get traffic to your site. The bottom line is the more places that have links to your site the higher the probability that someone is going to see them.

I know it's a lot of work. It can be difficult to stay motivated when getting traffic seems very slow. But be persistent and you will see that your hard work at marketing your blog will pay off in the long run.

Search Engine Optimization

When posting recipe photos, make sure to post the final image at the top of your post. This is important for SEO.

Search Engine Optimization is the process of using certain tactics to help a website rank better in the search engine listings. Writing post headlines with search engine listings in mind and using those same words from the headline in the body text help with search engine optimization. Tagging and linking your posts benefit you as well when it comes to this.

Obviously the more links into your site, the better. But it is important to note that some sites rank better than others. So, for example, if a blogger friend of yours links to your blog that is okay. But if the Huffington Post links to you, that is an authority site and has a lot more clout with the search engines than just another blog.

Mastering the Long Tail

The Long Tail is a unique or niche phrase. Rather than it just being two or three words it may be six or seven very specific words. As you might guess, this is very specific and not a phrase that most people are looking for. So why would you want to bother trying to rank or get found for a phrase that is a niche and doesn't drive much traffic?

As we know competition for popular keywords is fierce. So, trying to rank for "Top Seafood Restaurant Philadelphia" might be very difficult to get. But you might be able to rank well for "Barbecue Octopus in Philadelphia." While these niches might not bring a ton of traffic by themselves, having lots of niches of these Long Tail keywords collectively could really benefit your traffic.

How can you choose the Long Tail Keywords

As I said earlier, stick to about five to seven words. If the phrase includes a famous person or well known product be sure to include that in the title. Be as specific as possible and if your article is a "How to" include that in the title as people love to read and often search for how to articles.

A goldmine of keyword information can be found using the free Google Keyword tool. Just do a search for Google Keyword tool. Type in a phrase of about three to five words and see what results come up. The tool will demonstrate how different words and phrases rank and how popular they are. You might be surprised at what a change in traffic a slight change in word structure can do to search results.

Of course you don't have to make every article you write be in the structure that the Keyword tool recommends to get you the most traffic. Sometimes throwing in a phrase that is attention getting works well too. For example, I live in Atlanta, Georgia where the popular television show, The Walking Dead is filmed. Georgia is also known as the Peach State. When I was writing about a Walking Dead viewing party, the temptation might be to title the post "Walking Dead Viewing Party at Taylor's Pub." However, I went with the title "Eat Peaches, Not People." The intriguing title caused more people to click through and have it be shared than the more boring title.

Stats

It is very important to check your stats and see what articles and keywords are bringing people to your blog. It is always surprising to me what has brought people to my site. Some of the highest ranked posts are: A recipe I shared about Ribs, An Article about Great Fist Date Ideas, and a Dinner and Movie theatre restaurant.

Install Google Analytics (it is free) to keep track of your site and monitor traffic sources, demographics and what are popular posts.

Another important tracking feature is to install a Google Alert for you on your blog. You will need a google account. Go to google.com/alerts. You can set it to send you an email whenever there is a mention for your blog.

More terms

Anchor text: Anchor texts are the words that are used in a link that is clickable. It is important to have proper anchor text for backlinks that deal with the main theme of your article or site. For example, if your blog is about vegetarian recipes, having those words in backlinks helps your rank within google. Search engines will associate these keywords with the content of your website.

Backlink: This is a hyperlink on another website pointing back to your own website. They help with the PageRank and influencing your rank in the search engine listings. Having an inbound link from another site is like a vote for the site.

Duplicate Content: This is content that appears on different websites exactly word for word. This is never a good practice as search engines punish you by ranking your site lower in results if they see the same content on another site.

Keyword Stuffing: Part of a site or page ranking in search engines is that the search term matches what is on the site or page. Some webmasters had started to put a lot of the same keywords throughout the site or page, known as "stuffing" so the site would rank higher in the search engines. So, instead of keywords being sprinkled throughout the site, they are overused which often leads to getting penalized because it is essentially trying to trick the search engines.

Linkbait: A linkbait is content published on a website whose goal is to get as many backlinks as possible. While it can be written content, it is sometimes a video or image. Infographics have become very popular for this as everyone loves to share these images.

NoFollow: Just as a backlink from one site to another is an endorsement for that site, if a site owner makes the link a "nofollow" link they are telling search engines they don't vote for that site. This could happen when the link is for a sponsor or advertiser. When Google sees the nofollow attribute it discounts that link for the PageRank and search algorithms.

PageRank: PageRank is based on an algorithm that Google uses to estimate the importance of pages on the internet. The more inbound links a site has, the better. It creates the idea of more importance to the search engines, which rank it higher in listings.

Search Algorithm: Google's search algorithm is a mathematical formula used to find the most relevant content when any search term is entered. According to Google, there are over 200 factors considered in determining this. PageRank value, the title tag, the website content, how old the domain is and so on.

SEM: Stands for Search Engine Marketing, and as the name implies it involves marketing through search engines. There are two types of SEM -- PPC and SEO. You already know SEO is Search Engine Optimization. PPC stands for Pay-Per-Click, and it is the practice of buying clicks from search engines via ads. The clicks come from sponsored listings in the search results.

SERP: Search Engine Results Page. It's basically the page you'll get when you search for a specific keyword on Google or on other search engines. The amount of search traffic your website will receive depends on the rankings it will have inside the SERPs.

Title Tag: The title tag is literally the title of a web page, and it's one of the most important factors inside Google's search algorithm. Ideally your title tag should be unique and contain the main keywords of your page. You can see the title tag of any web page on top of the browser while navigating it.

Web Crawler: Also called search spider, they scour the web for search engines, looking for new content. This is how search engines find the content to add to their database of results for any given term.

Chapter 7 – Social Media

One of the very first things, you read in this book is that Social Media will play a huge role in getting readership. Here is insight into many of these sites and how to use them to your advantage.

In the beginning it is quite overwhelming how many social media profiles there are for you to use. Make sure to secure your name on each one as they become available. Even if you don't use them as much as others, at least get the name so no one else can take it.

With auto publishing, it is easy to get your content published to Facebook and Twitter. Using Wordpress, you can install plugins, so it should be a no-brainer to set these up. And you can easily link both Foursquare and Instagram to Twitter so get those up quickly.

Facebook is one of the oldest and still the largest social networking platforms around. You definitely want to use Facebook to your advantage. People spend hours a day on Facebook. Did you know if it was a country, it would be the third largest country in the world?

Get your Facebook page setup. Make sure it is a fan page and not a profile page like your personal page. Put your logo or an image of you as the small image and make the cover image a pretty image of food. Remember that branding we talked about? That's where these images come in.

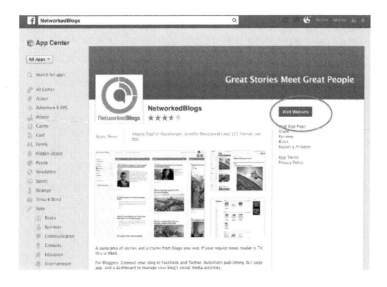

Always post your new articles to Facebook. Autopublish if possible. The app is called Networked blogs that will allow you to autopublish to Facebook. Install it onto your Facebook personal profile as well. Your friends should be interested in what you are writing about too!

It will then give you a snippet to put into your blog to verify that you are indeed the owner. Once the site is verified, you can remove the code. You may want to tag restaurants in your posts as well. Note that this feature is not available with autoposting. For this you'll need to manually add the link to your post.

Beyond simply publishing your own posts share interesting posts by other bloggers and restaurant happenings. Facebook isn't limited to just a fan page and sharing. Network, network, network. Friend your fellow bloggers. Keep connected to them and see what they are up to. It is inspirational to keep up with them and what they are writing about on a regular basis.

Twitter – Again make sure to use your logo as your avatar. No one wants to follow someone with the egg shape avatar. Twitter feeds update like crazy, so you always want to make sure you are instantly recognizable. There's a battle to be seen and heard in Social media and you want to make sure you do everything possible to get that done.

Just like Facebook you can autopublish your blog posts to Twitter, but I recommend against it. Here's why: the plugin will only publish posts like this:

Example Tweet 1 - {new post} Review of Dusty's Barbecue www.atlantarestaurantblog/review-dustys-barbecue.

As compared to

Example Tweet 2 - Brisket, wings and the Hawgarita – must haves @dustysbarbecue bit.ly.atlr786 #wings #barbecue #ATLdining

It is better than nothing and if you simply don't have the time to handle all the tweets yourself than certainly go this route. I recommend tweeting yourself if you can. This way, you can take the time to craft your own message with unique hashtags. Between the tweets above which one sounds more interesting?

A few things to note about twitter.

Anyone who follows you can see your tweets. But you can't DM (direct message someone) who isn't following you.

If you start a tweet with @soandso it may not be seen by everyone. If you want others to see it put a "." In front of the @ symbol.
Hashtags - Creative hashtags are great. Hashtags are subject identifies. Some groups have twitter chats in which they use their own hashtag or a certain event may designate a hashtag. While, no one can own a hashtag they are useful in that anyone can search twitter for these. So when you write your post about Vietnamese food you might want to use the hashtag #VietnameseRecipe. Note that symbols cannot be used in hashtags, only letters.

YouTube
If there is one social media platform that bloggers are not taking advantage of, but should, it is YouTube. Did you know that YouTube is the second largest search engine? It is owned by Google. Ever search for something on google and have several of the results on the first page be a Youtube video? Doesn't that little image just make you want to click on it more?

Now, you may be thinking:
I'm not a professional videographer.
I don't know about shooting and editing video.
I got into this blogging thing because I like to write – I don't want to get involved in video.

But if you really look at most of the videos you see on Youtube they aren't professional quality. If you work on a Mac there is a program called iMovie that makes it super easy to create videos. If you don't there is a free service called Animoto where you can use pictures and small video clips to create your very own professional looking movies.

Really, most bloggers are not taking advantage of this traffic-getting resource so YOU absolutely should. And don't misunderstand the difference between content and quality. Sure, it helps if the video is professionally done, but if the content is exceptional people won't care so much about the quality.

Another reason to start engaging in Youtube? They have an ad area specifically to connect brands directly with those influencers they might work well with: http://www.youtube.com/yt/creators/

Yelp – Ah Yelp. I, like many bloggers, have a love / hate relationship with Yelp. Don't you just love the "reviewers" that give a restaurant one star because the hostess gave them a funny look? As a user of Yelp I do like it for a consensus about a restaurant. Any savvy reviewer knows you should read at least a good handful if not all of the reviews before deciding to eat or not eat at a restaurant based on Yelp.

That being said, Yelp is a good way to get traffic to your site. You can take advantage of Yelp in several ways:

When you fill out your profile you are asked to list your blog or website or favorite site. Duh! Put your blog in there. However, most people are not going to click on your profile right away.
So make sure to put a link to the post about the restaurant in your Yelp review. Your longer full review should be on your blog for several days before you change up and shorten the post about a restaurant on Yelp. Remember, in the beginning it is important you do everything you can to get your name out there and traffic to your site. Using large sites like Yelp helps tremendously.

Pictures – Everyone wants to see pictures. Like the old saying goes, a picture is worth a thousand words. So, go on and upload some pictures (1 or 2) to the restaurant review. Of course you will want to put the majority on your blog, but sharing a couple good pictures is a way of establishing yourself. You want people to seek out your reviews on Yelp and then as you become better known, just visit your blog.

Yelp and Branding – While I harp on about branding, in this case, I don't recommend putting your logo as your profile pic on Yelp. Yelp's motto is "Real People. Real Reviews." You want to seem as real as possible and putting a logo sort of negates that. So put a picture of yourself. If you are trying to stay anonymous, pick a cartoon logo or some image that you feel is a good representation of your blog and use that.

Yelp Events – Yelp users are always looking for something to do. Especially on the weekends. So, why not use the information you are getting in those newsletters that you signed up for and post events on Yelp. Users will be grateful you did and restaurants will be happy for the added exposure. Most will never think of doing this themselves.

You may be wondering if Yelp is averse in any way to posting outbound links, and currently the answer is no. I've posted about many events around my city, and linked to my blog directly in the writeup and have never gotten any pushback from Yelp.

Urban Spoon
Similar to Yelp, Urbanspoon is a review site. The different thing about Urbanspoon vs. Yelp is that they have a separate area for bloggers. Reviews are categorized as either a Critic, Bloggers or User Review. The way Urbanspoon words is to give you a code for each blog post that you can put in the post.

Each city has a blogger leaderboard on Urbanspoon. This is based on how many clickthroughs you get to read your reviews. There are two strategies. Obviously quantity counts. If you have hundreds of reviews you will get more clickthroughs than someone with only 30 reviews. However, there is another way to increase clickthroughs: review a popular restaurant.

For each city, Urban Spoon lists the top 10 restaurants which they refer to as the Talk of the Town. These change often but if you can regularly write about at least one or two of the restaurants in the top 10, you will get more clickthroughs as they are the restaurants that are hot right now.

While I don't want to put too much emphasis on climbing the Urbanspoon ladder, it does show a lot of clout to be in the top 10. You will have to evaluate for your city what makes sense for you to do. If you live in Seattle, San Francisco or New York for example, there are so many bloggers it will be difficult for you to break into the top 10. However, a smaller city such as Charlotte or Louisville, or Tulsa, you might be able to do that quite easily.

My recommendation is work the strategy – quantity and popularity. That combination is the best way for climbing up the ladder. However, if you live in a heavily blogger populated city don't spend all your time trying to break into the top

10. Also, if you aren't in the top 10 don't put the badge on your blog.

Picture sharing sites:
Pinterest – a virtual board where users can create their very own boards on different subjects and upload their own pictures and share other photos. Many bloggers say that they get the most traffic from pinterest. This is especially important for recipe bloggers.

Instagram, Foodgawker and Tastspotting – More photo sharing sites that can get you traffic for your blog. Instagram (a photo editing platform) is nice because you can share the content to Facebook and Twitter.

Forums
We talked about forums briefly. They should be easy enough to find. Just go to google and type in "your city food forum" and some sites should come up. Make sure to include your blog link in your signature. Always be helpful and contribute in any comments on the forum you make. NEVER just post a link to your blog. It will anger users and they won't respect you.

The other thing to keep in mind about forums is this: some of those people are bat sh*t crazy! I remember once I was in a forum and posted something about a meal I had and I meant to type "basil" but mistakenly wrote "cilantro" instead. Those people jumped all over me! So, approach it knowing that you need a thick skin. Remember people are willing to be a lot nastier and unkind when they are hiding behind a computer and their true identity will never be revealed.

Other Bloggers
I have gotten so much pleasure from the friends I've made through food blogging. It is so terrific to know that so many people are just like me and will travel long distances for a fantastic slice of pizza or gyro or lobster roll, etc, etc.

One thing that has surprised me with many of the bloggers I've met is that they have a completely different personality in real life than they do online. Have you encountered this? This mostly comes from Twitter. Even though it is only words, no matter what - any person, business, or organization has a personality.

You should strive to make your online personality consistently match who you really are. I think many writers are naturally introverted. I am. So, if you want to come off with strong opinions, be ready to discuss them or be challenged on them when you meet other bloggers. I've been surprised by so many bloggers who have strong personalities on Twitter but when they are challenged in public they just clam up.

Or worse, I don't understand the ones who have a big personality online, yet when they are at a media event or tweetup, they don't talk to anyone but simply play on their smartphone. Social media is a great traffic getter and an important part to building your brand, but that cannot replace human interaction. So put the phone down and get to know your fellow bloggers and develop a relationship with them.

Naturally, there will be some that you like more than others and develop a camaraderie with. Not only do you provide a support system to one another but encourage each other to keep writing, try new restaurants together and share blogging tips and resources. They may refer you for a writing job. OR you never know if a business partnership could develop from this. This has happened for many bloggers I've met as well as for me over the years.

Free Publiciy – Most bloggers find this one a little tricky. It is quite difficult to make a name for yourself quickly if you are relatively unknown. If you are a bit shy like me, it is even more difficult to step up and really be the attention-getting kind.

However, I still tried it and recommend you do, too. Here's what I did: At the time I started by blog, the movie Slumdog Millionaire was very popular. Do you remember how almost everyone was talking about it? I was born in India but lived the first 5 weeks of my life in an orphanage, narrowly escaping death. I tied that experience into a Press Release entitled "Atlanta's Own Slumdog Millionaire."

While you may not have that dramatic of a story to tell, you do have a story. YOU have a hook – I know it! Think about what events have happened in your life and relate to current events going on today. Even if the tie in is somewhat weak, you can make a story out of it. The story is what sells the piece.

The Press loves human interest stories. Start with a great hook and then answer the questions who, what where, why and when and how. If you can answer these questions in the body of your release, you'll definitely have a lot to talk about. If you have trouble coming up with a hook, ask friends or family members to help you come up with one as they know you best.

Remember the catchy headline is what will grab a reporter's attention. While it may not have gotten me on the local news, I did get some mentions from it and was even asked to write a couple pieces for a local magazine because my story was so moving. Of course, I had blog articles written that showed my expertise.

Some other ideas for generating interest in your release:

Be opinionated – if you have a strong opposing opinion to a hot story (and can back it up with reason and facts) go for it!

Provide stats – reporters love stats

Solve a problem – this is the best way to get press coverage. Your blog solves a problem for people – where to eat, what to cook. Is there a way to frame that into a story to promote to the media?

Chapter 8 – Networking

Many of us dread networking as it relates to job searching. But it doesn't have to be horrible if you take the right steps to prepare for networking at different foodie events.

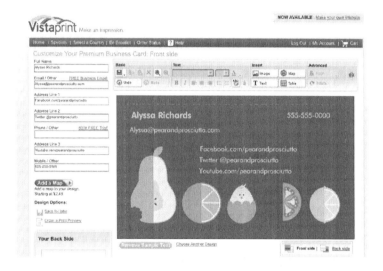

Get business cards

You can get these done rather cheaply via Vistaprint.com and if you have a logo to use pay the extra money to get that on your card. Instead of a mailing address, put in your social media links: Facebook / Twitter / Youtube / Pinterest.

Dress the part

Many people think of food bloggers as hipsters who hang around in coffee shops, banging away on their keyboards, wearing jeans and a t-shirt. Dispel this myth. Dress up when you show up at events, no matter what everyone else is wearing. It shows you respect your host and people pay you more respect than you think.

Meetings

Not sure what meeting organizations are available for blogges in your community? A great place to start is with Meetup groups. There are Meetup groups for any number of subjects. While there may not be a group for food bloggers specifically, there may be one for bloggers in general. Join and go to one meeting. They are free and you never know what you may learn or what connections you will make.

Clubs and Organizations

Besides the Association of Food Bloggers which is an international membership organization, many cities have sprung up with their own food blogger groups. These are a great benefit to bloggers starting out to learn the ins and outs of blogging as they are usually started by seasoned bloggers.

By joining one of these organizations, you will probably get invitations to some media events because of the clout of the organization. Some will require dues or a certain criteria to be a member, but try to join as soon as possible because these organizations, when run well, can propel you a lot further faster than going it alone.

PR events

Two of the most exciting words to bloggers are: "You're Invited." We all love to see those two words in the subject line of an email. Publicity events mostly consist of being plied with booze and an overabundance of food in an effort to get you to write about a restaurant.

When you are just starting out as a blogger, you need to get a feel for who the movers and shakers are in your city. I don't just mean the big PR companies, but also bloggers that are heavy influencers. Those are the people you want to rub elbows with. So, my advice is to go to EVERYTHING you get invited to in the beginning. When you start to get a feel for whether a PR company is going to put on a good event or not, you can choose to go or not to go.

But I recommend waiting until you are pretty well established in your community before doing this.

Remember, you need content for your blog and this is a great way to get it. I suggest you tweet / instragram while you are the event using the relevant hashtag if there is one. This shows your importance and users will take note. So, will other PR companies.

Etiquette

Show up on time. Sometimes events start on time, sometimes they don't. But you don't want to be the rude guest who shows up 30 minutes after it's underway.

Post in a timely manner. Make sure to post as soon as you can. Most bloggers will wait about a week to post after an event. Get the jump on them and be the first to report about a new restaurant. Not only does it show that you are in the know, but you can use this to your advantage as being one of the first to post on Urbanspoon.

Bring one guest if allowed. None if not allowed. PR companies are all different. But remember they are at the mercy of the restaurant. Some will allow you to bring a "plus one" to a media dinner, some won't. They usually tell you if you can bring a guest in the initial email, but if they don't, it is okay to ask. Whatever response you get, respect that. Don't show up with your "photographer" who also happens to be your girlfriend/ boyfriend. They see right through that.

I cannot stress enough how important it is to build relationships. The relationships you build with others will help you get to other goals. Although I was a published author and well-respected blogger, it wasn't because of either of those things that got me to be a judge at our city's annual food festival. It was because I was a friend with their Social Media Director that led me to this.

Every person you meet is a possible connection to get you to your next goal or you next project. I'm certainly not advocating that you use people to get what you want, absolutely not! Be kind and helpful and in return you will get the same from others. Keep up good relationships too. Make it a point to have lunch or dinner with colleagues. Not only is it good networking but it is also good for you to encourage each other to keep blogging and discuss issues that you've had with blogging.

Chapter 9 --Ethics

To quote Dr. Frasier Crane "Ethics are what you do when no one else is looking."

Disclosure - According to the FTC, by law you must disclose freebies that you are given. Besides durables like books or cooking utensils, this includes any free meals that you are given. It is just part of our ethical standards, and, well, the right thing to do. So, if you are reviewing a restaurant based on a free meal, you should be disclosing (somewhere in the post) that you received the meal for free. However, the FTC made it law that bloggers much disclose such freebies just over a year or so ago.

Did you know that this extends to even Facebook and Twitter? And there are hefty fines (up to $11,000) if found guilty of non-disclosure. View the full guidelines on the FTC website if you need more details. It gives the FTC free reign to investigate anyone, who endorses a product if the FTC finds that the product was anything other than a cash for product / service transaction.

So why is the FTC targeting bloggers more than others? They point to the fact of the power and clout of blogs. This stealthy Social Media Marketing could convince someone to unknowingly purchase a good or service that was a paid endorsement. In 2007, the blog-for-profit sector was worth $1.35 million according to Word of Mouth Marketing. We surmise that this is mostly aimed at electronic goods (think mobile phones, video games, mp3 players and more). Of course, food bloggers are not exempt.

The best advice, based on what we know, is that it is worth it to write somewhere in post "Full Disclosure: This was a free meal provided by Abc restaurant."

While we firmly believe in disclosure – you wouldn't want to buy a car based on a paid endorsement from a blogger would you? – We believe no one should be exempt from this disclosure. Only time will tell how these new laws will play out and what impact they will truly have.

Honesty

Besides disclosing the fact that you receive free meals or free tools for cooking, honesty is the best policy. Always. What we mean is, don't fib if you don't like something. Of course, you don't have to rip it apart, but just give you true feedback. If you do like something, don't gush. Be positive, but don't gush on and on about it. Of course, the old adage, If you don't have anything nice to say don't say anything at all, is good advice.

Credit Sources

Bloggers are a funny bunch. Even if you are good friends, that doesn't mean what's mine is yours. If you want to use their pictures or something from their blog, you need to credit them. Also, it is good practice to site sources for images that you may use. Don't want to do that? You can always get royalty free images. Some sources for these are:

istockPhoto.com
Thinkstockphotos.com
GettyImages.com

These are just a few places to get royalty free images. You will have to pay a small fee to use the images, but it is good to have the peace of mind that you are fully abiding by the law by using these images. Of course the best thing to do is take your own photos.

Protecting Your Content

Even if you wouldn't take someone else's photograph what if they took yours? The sad part of all information being available free online is that sometimes people take others' content without permission. So how do you protect your content online? Put a copyright notice at the bottom of your page. This will serve as a notice that your content is not free for the taking, though that should be understood.

With regard to recipes, I'm not a lawyer and am not qualified to dispense legal advice, but here's what I can share with you: you can't protect your ingredients list but you can copyright the methodology.

With photography, I recommend putting a watermark on your photographs. While there is nothing you can do if someone takes it and crops it, they might think twice if they see a copyright notice.

Be vigilant and give people the benefit of the doubt. If you see your content elsewhere message them and ask them to take it down. After that, there isn't much you can do other than hiring an attorney to send them a cease and desist notice.

Chapter 10 -- Photography

If you aren't proficient with the web and social media, it isn't too hard to learn for yourself. However, there is a learning curve involved. If you are already familiar with photography you are ahead of many other bloggers. Though it isn't mandatory, you may find it worthwhile to buy a DLR camera and invest in a course about using it.

Here are some tips for picture taking using a smartphone or point and shoot:

Light –- this is your best asset when it comes to great picture taking. If there is daylight whether inside our outdoors, this will help you to take the best pictures possible. Using a flash almost always diminishes the quality of a photo that you could have had with true daylight. Also avoid any kind of incandescent light. An overhead lamp or any bright bulb that is in your picture will take away from your subject.

If you have a regular point and shoot camera, the flash will almost always be overpowering for food. Try taking a paper napkin and folding it over the flash. This has a dulling effect on the flash. Although it is still needed, the light is dimmed so the food doesn't look completely washed out.

Here's another trick, but it only works if you are dining with a friend who also has a phone. Have them hold their phone so the light from it lights up a dish. Then take your photo without any flash. This will give the lighting effect necessary to show the food but won't be too overpowering.

Instagram is your best friend. Perhaps you already know the power of editing with Instagram. There are about a dozen different filters you can add to your photo.

Size – While the size of an entrée may seem very obvious to you when it is right in front of you, a picture betrays that. So, when trying to show how large or small a particular item is, place something that everyone knows the size of near it.

What you see is what you get.
When taking a picture, we all know that you can edit later. But perhaps there is a part of the menu (the restaurant name) or if you are working on a recipe perhaps there is a tool that you wanted in the picture. When viewing these images through your camera make sure to take note of any extraneous objects that are also in the picture. Is a dirty fork in there or a crumpled up napkin? These are things you wouldn't want in the picture and may not be easy to crop if there are other objects (like a glass of wine next to it) that you did want in the picture.

Other tips:

Resolution –- Your camera has various resolution settings. Make sure that it is on the highest resolution for food photography. Although it isn't obvious when you view the picture on your phone, you will notice that a low resolution image will look blurry on your computer.

Be a shutterbug –- It can be frustrating when you are out with friends at a restaurant and the food is brought to the table and everyone just wants to dig in. So, it can be tempting to just snap a picture and put your phone away. Of course there are moments when it is appropriate to only take one picture (like at a special celebration). But in other circumstances take several pictures of the food at different angles. You never know which angle will turn out to the best one. Plus, when you take many pictures, you will know better for next time what angle or lighting situation, etc. works best.

Stability

When using a flash, stability is not much of an issue. However, stability is crucial when you are using low light. If you aren't using a flash, hold the camera as steady as possible to ensure a clear image.

If at all possible hold the camera on a ledge or on the table when taking pictures so there is no shake. Shaking will result in a blurry image. If nothing is available to use as a ledge, try holding the camera with both hands as close to your upper body as possible, which will help to stabilize the shot.

Capture experiences

As much as it is terrific to only take pictures of dishes, some of the best restaurant photos don't have food in it at all. They just show a table of people laughing and having a good time. If you are at a media event, it may be that it is quite acceptable to go into the kitchen or take a picture of the chef at work. Go and capture that experience to share with your readers.

Remember you are using pictures to convey a general feel for the restaurant. Of course you want to show off some of the best dishes, but don't forget that a big part of eating out is the ambience and the feel of the restaurant. So make sure you try as much as you can to capture that and share with your readers.

Chapter 11 – Dealing with PR companies

So many publicists out there frustrate me. But don't tell them I said that! Many come across overly sweet and totally fake. But it is the nature of the beast. The way it usually works is there are a handful of companies that work for the majority of the restaurants in any city or town.

As bloggers, there's a thrill of excitement we all get when two little words pop into an email in our inbox: "You're Invited." It is an exciting thing to be invited to media events, especially in the beginning. But it all comes at a price. Public relations professionals have a responsibility to provide coverage for their clients. That is where you, the blogger, come in. After talking to many public relations professionals, we've put together this list of ways bloggers can aggravate public relations professionals and guarantee no future invites from them.

1. Can I bring my photographer, who also happens to be my SO?

You may think you are being clever, asking to bring your "photographer" with you. But most publicists see right through that. If you have a plus one, that's cool, just disclose it ahead of time. "We do make every effort to accommodate the extra person, but please understand we are at the mercy of the restaurant," Atlanta Publicist Kitsy Rose says. If we say only media, then it is only media. You may slip by us once with the "plus one" angle, but we'll remember you next time.

2. Not writing in a timely manner

"If we invite you to an event for a preview – guess what? That means we want you to write about it BEFORE the event takes place. Three months after doesn't really help us out. In fact, while we are on the subject, if it takes you more than three months to write about out event we've most likely already written you off, especially if you are a new blogger we are working with."

3. Feeling entitled

I hear this from publicists all the time: Bloggers are invited to a restaurant and ask to bring numerous friends with them. The norm is you can bring one person to events or one guest when you are reviewing a restaurant. Ask for more, and you come across greedy and entitled.

4. Being a No Show

You committed to showing up. You need to do what you say. If for some reason you can't make it email or call and let us know. We might be able to give someone else your slot. It doesn't matter if something better came along. Keep in mind that this relationship is for the long haul not just a free meal for a midweek night.

5. Don't skip the tip

This should go without saying but if you were invited to dine somewhere, you are getting a complimentary meal, so leave a good tip! If the gathering is a true media event with many of your peers, often times tipping is not necessary. But when you and a guest are invited to a restaurant for a review with a "comped" meal, a tip is customary. Many PR companies inform you of this beforehand. If the invitation came directly from a restaurant, it is likely they won't ask you to do this, but it is expected.

6. Honest Feedback

Yep. Public Relations do want your feedback. To them. Not to the public. This is a tricky one. You can't fib on your reviews to keep getting invites.

You need to provide valuable, honest content for your readers. Yet if you pan numerous clients, chances are you won't get more invites from a particular PR company.

So what is a blogger to do? For the most part, it is almost always possible to find the good in a restaurant experience. Maybe only one appetizer was disappointing or out of two entrees, one really out-shined another. Focus more on those, even if you do mention the less than perfect dishes. You can share the full details of the negatives with the publicist.

A publicist's job is to make the restaurant look better to the public. And restaurants do hold them accountable for freebies. Publicist's use bloggers and other media to help spread the word about new dining establishments. But keep in mind this is a relationship both sides should nurture, not abuse.

7. Don't Rant on Social Media

Many bloggers are guilty of this: Not filling out a request for media passes to a food festival, etc, then emailing a publicist a day or two before the event and asking for media passes. It is not surprising when they don't respond. They are swamped with all the last minute details.

The last thing you should do is add to that stress. If you didn't get a response to your email and it is urgent then give them a call. But don't get on Twitter and say something nasty because they didn't get back to you to fulfill your request after you chose not to follow their protocol.

Chapter 12 -- Monetization

So you've done all this work – site design, content writing, branding, social media establishment, networking and now you are ready to monetize your site. This is purposely almost at the end of this book, because it is imperative to focus on these other elements as the foundation for a good blog. After you've done that, you can shift your attention to monetization.

There are several different ways you can go about monetizing your blog: Advertising, Bartering, Ad Networks, Adsense, and Affiliate products. We'll discuss all the options in this chapter.

Advertising

Remember, in the fist chapter when we discussed pages, you added a page on Advertising? This page serves as your media kit. With all of your stats, including social media followers, etc. a potential advertiser has everything needed to make a decision whether to advertise with you or not. Advertising on websites can take place via banner ads which are the most common or text advertising, which shows text embedded into an article or post.

One thing you'll always want to keep in mind is that content should come first and advertising second. Advertising should blend into the fantastic content that you are providing your readers. If you are talking about a superb blender that you used in a recipe, that is the perfect time to include a link to sell it. This is what is called an affiliate link, which is described in more detail below. Keep in mind how important it is to keep your advertising blended in with your content. Always provide fantastic content, but don't ever forget about the fact that you need to make money.

Don't get too excited over the banner ad monetization method. I wanted to tell you about it so you know what it is, but it is rather unlikely that a major brand will contact you directly about advertising. Why? Most large brands advertise through Ad networks, which we will discuss later in this chapter.

However, it is possible that a local business might want to advertise on your blog. Start cheap at about $25 per banner ad per month. While you won't want to reach out to restaurants as that wouldn't be fair since you are reviewing restaurants, you could advertise companies that would be of complimentary interest to your readers. A cooking school would be a great fit.

Many foodies have pets. So maybe you could advertise a pet hotel or perhaps there is a local theatre that could use some advertising. Just try to keep in mind businesses that would be a good fit for your demographic.

Ads come in all sizes but remember the specifications you set in your media kit. You want to do this because you will be using plugins to add ads to your site. Here are the two I've used and recommend:

Max Banner Ads
125 x 125 plugin

Both are free and are easy to customize. Once you activate the plugins, it is just a matter of uploading the image file. Remember, it is up to the customer to supply this image to you. They can either email you an image file that you can upload or they can provide you with the link in which the image is stored. You'll then simply add the destination link of where the ad should take visitors when they click on the link. Both of these plugins provide tracking so you can keep count of how many impressions and clicks the ads provided.

Make sure to be clear to the customer that you will put the banner up on your blog, but it is up to them to provide you with a banner design.

There are other plugins that you can research and play around with to find what suits your style and your blog best, but these are two good one to get started.

Barter

I love the idea of bartering for goods and services. I think it's an idea that should never have gone out of style. Bartering isn't exactly monetization but it is a good way to exchange for goods that you would want. Think of your favorite restaurant. While I wouldn't normally recommend advertising a restaurant (it can appear like a conflict of interest especially if you are reviewing it) you can make an exception for them and add a banner ad to your site. In exchange you can get a dining credit with them.

Some other places you can barter with are people that provide services to you on a regular basis. Perhaps you could barter with your dentist? They are always looking for new patients and almost everyone makes it a habit to visit the dentist regularly. You could barter for your cleanings.

What about your hair salon? Hair salons are all over the place and always need new clientele. You could exchange salon services for an ad on your blog as well.

Of course, these businesses will expect some ROI, so be prepared to give them a free trial for a month to see how well it works. While you may not exactly make money from bartering, you are saving money as you don't have to pay for some of these common expenses. Also, since I am not a tax expert, you should check with your tax accountant as to how to handle the entire area of bartering.

Google Adsense

You've probably seen those Google Adsense banners on lots of websites and other blogs. They are vertical ads which are text. They are some of the easiest to install on a website or blog. Register and get a snippet of code to add to your blog. People place those ads with Google and then Google matches those ads with sites that have content relevant to the ads.

The way it works is that you get a small amount of change whenever someone clicks on one of those links. The problem is that it is a small amount. It could be as little as $0.02 per click. So it would take a lot of clicks to make any substantial amount of money. But it's still worth it.

Amazon

With the Amazon model, you get a small percentage of the sale whenever someone buys a product that you have listed for sale. Amazon does a great job of giving you lots of images, banners, text ads and widgets to install to make it as easy as possible to integrate the products into your blog posts.

You can even have your own Amazon store setup. This would be your Amazon page with all the products you recommend that others buy. You can simply link to this page from you blog or put it in a post. Again, the percentage per sale is rather small – think ($0.50) on a $15 product.
Ad networks

Ad networks work by offering ads by large companies. Have you often noticed that you see the same ad displayed on many other blogs? It is because they are part of the same ad network. This is usually measured by how many impressions your ad gets. Again you are paid a small amount for this.

Unless your blog has huge traffic numbers – like over six figure stats per month, you will have to use ad networks or one of the other models above. Pitching a huge brand won't work as they choose to work with ad networks, where they get their product advertised on many blogs and only have to pay a small amount.

Affiliate Marketing

For sites with not a lot of traffic, affiliate marketing is probably the best way to make sales. Affiliate marketing is when a company pays someone for selling their products. Usually this is an electronic product. E-books and plugins and different tools can be sold like this through affiliate marketing.

The good thing is you serve as a pass through, once the person buys the product on another site they handle all the billing and collection of funds. Even if there is a refund, they handle that as well. All you are doing is helping to sell the product.

Of course, you want to make sure you choose a reputable company to do business with. One of the ones that has been around the longest and is well trusted is Clickbank. They are a marketplace for affiliate products and sell all types of these products.

Another thing that is nice about these products is that the revenue share is high. Instead of say, 1 percent of the sale or something pithy like Adsense or Amazon, Clickbank products offer about 50 percent or more. If an ebook is $50 and you sell it, making 50 percent, that's $25 bucks!

However, there is more work involved in selling these products than say a product on Amazon. With Amazon, many of the products they are selling may be products that your reader has seen before or knows about and perhaps just needs a nudge to buy it.

With Clickbank, you are likely trying to sell them a product that they weren't aware of before. You have to do a little more work than just listing a product image or text link on your blog. Reviews of products work well for affiliate marketing. So, you will need to test the product out and make sure it works well if you are doing that.

And if you can do a review with a video that shows you using the product that works even better.

Besides or in addition to Clickbank you can try:
Commission Junction
Pay Dot Com

Here's what is important to remember with selling affiliate products: you need to have a general understanding of the problem that the product solves. If you simply slap up a quick review that is nothing more than a sales pitch, your readers won't believe you have used the product and won't be inclined to buy it. Sadly, that is what most bloggers do and then are surprised when they don't make any sales.

The best way to start selling affiliate products is to start with low prices, products under $100. Anything higher and you audience might find it hard to commit to the price point. Make sure the products are a good fit for you and your style. For example, if you write a lot about baking, trying to sell grilling products probably wouldn't be a good fit.

Your goal should be to show both /the product's assets and its flaws. Simply writing a glowing review isn't going to sell the product. If you write restaurant reviews you probably follow this same mantra, also. Doing a comparison review of several products is a great way to sell affiliate products. For example, you could do a comparison of three different mixers and give the positives and negatives of all three.

The end of the review is the clincher. Focus on the ideal situation of the buyer – what problem does the product solve? What other resources does the buyer need? How much more research or education will they need before they can implement the product. Are they in the right financial situation to buy this product? If this person can identify with the exact situation of your reader, they will be inclined to purchase it.

Make sure you title your post with the word "review" in it. That way when people are looking for reviews about a product you've reviewed, it will come up in the search engines.

Of course reviews mixed in with others in posts get buried. So it is good practice to have a page on your blog of all the reviews you've done, so readers can peruse it. Also, make sure to link to review posts in future articles whenever relevant.

Even if you sell a product that makes $25 a sale, getting an arsenal of 100 of these could add up to a decent four figure income each month.

Sponsored Posts

Sponsored posts are becoming more and more popular. They are usually done in one of two ways. A company gives you a product to review and usually gives you payment for the review. Or they simply give you a prewritten review to post. It can be good money, but you need to be aware of your own credibility. If you sponsor a post for a lousy product, your audience won't be happy with you. I'll talk more about sponsored posts and the dangers with them in the next chapter.

Rates

Rates can vary greatly but a very rough estimate is 10 percent of the daily amount of visitors you have up to about 1,000 daily readers. If you have 500 readers per day, you should be able to get $50 for a text link or a banner campaign (roughly).

A blog with 5000 daily visitors can demand as much as $1,000 per month for a banner campaign and $250 for a text link.

Keeping up with payments

IF you have lots of advertisers both text ads and banner ads, you'll need to keep up with payment collection and when ads expire. I recommend keeping an excel spread sheet with all the details of ads and when they expire, that way you know when you need to chase after advertisers for payment.

Chapter 13 – Scams

There are all sorts of scams out there. And scammers have become much more sophisticated than the Nigerian Prince who wants to wire you 1.2 million dollars to help you out. Here are some of the scams that I have seen and dealt with over the past years of blogging.

Link Builders

As we talked about in previous chapters, inbound links into your site help your rank. The higher the quality site the better it is for the site that it links to. Once your site reaches a certain level (rank, page views, etc) you may start to notice people volunteer to write guest posts for you. However, instead of a guest post in which you choose the topic, it will mostly be a prewritten article on a topic that they have chosen. You'll notice they want to include a link to another site. This is because they are a link builder. They are paid to build inbound links to a site.

Unless the article is completely unrelated to the topics on your blog, it won't do any harm to add

the article to your blog. However, you will want to make sure of a few things:
The article is unique content – not duplicated all over other blogs. Having duplicated content will hurt your site.

The link is a no follow link. They probably won't like this, if the article is truly for link building. A no follow link in essence tells the search engine "this isn't a vote for this site."

Another sneaky way linkbuilders work is to offer you an infographic to include on your blog. The infographic contains a link on it. Again, it won't harm your site, but you would want to know that adding such an infographic is something that someone is being paid to get posted on numerous sites.

Plugins

Here's a scam that someone tried to pull on me: asking me to install a plugin on my blog that was malicious. You should never install a plugin that doesn't come from a trusted source. By installing a plugin, you are essentially giving that plugin access to your site. It is very similar to adding an app on your phone. It gives the app access to pretty much everything on your phone.

The best advice is to install plugins that come directly from Wordpress.org OR if there is a site that you follow and trust, then you can install the plugin. About two years ago, I was asked about advertising a banner ad on my blog. The company accepted my high price for advertising which was a clue this was a scam. But rather than supply an image file, they wanted me to install a plugin for the advertising. I refused, because it seemed like it was a scam. Plugins could install any sort of malicious content on your site. It could wipe your site clean or steal content, or any number of other things.

Sponsored Posts

You will probably be approached by companies representing products or services to pay you in order to write a post. This is a sponsored post and should be labeled as such. I've been asked to post a pre-written article in exchange for payment. The only catch is I've been asked to not disclose it was a sponsored post. Why? When you list something as a sponsored post, search engines instantly discredit and devalue it.
But if it is not something you wrote AND you are getting paid to post it, then it is clearly a sponsored post.

Not only is it unethical for you to post this without disclosing it. But your readers are accustomed to your tone and style and will know it isn't you writing and you can lose credibility. Not only that, there are laws about full disclosure.

You'll also waste a lot of time if you don't let any potential advertisers know this is your policy up front. I had 17 emails back and forth with an advertiser where they tried to convince me to publish their post without disclosing it was a sponsored post.

Safety

As much as we've talked about branding and not being afraid to show who you really are and not hide behind anything, be smart when it comes to you safety. When you share check-ins on Facebook, Twitter and Foursquare you are essentially telling the whole world where you are. While most of the people out there are harmless, you never know who is truly "following" you.

Be smart about sharing information. If you post a checkin to Facebook, Twitter or another Social Media outlet you are also notifying everyone that you are not at home. Be careful. The more unsafe thing, is being somewhere where you will have to walk back to your car by yourself I make it a policy if I am at an event somewhere, I only check-in after I am safely locked inside my car.

Conclusion

With following everything you read here in this book, you have the tools you need to become a successful blogger. But as you can see from reading, there is quite a bit of work involved in getting your blog known, popular and with lots of traffic but it can be done.
Stay persistent no matter what your goal is. And remember your goal may shift from one thing to another.

For me, I thought I would get a huge amount of traffic and sell advertising on my blog. Instead, some of my readers became clients. It turned out that my blog is a conduit for getting business. I write blogs professionally and manage social media profiles and between my readers and all the networking events I go to, I meet lots of potential clients.

Perhaps you may become a consultant, advising businesses on social media and bloggers. Or perhaps you may become a recipe developer or start a non-profit. All of these are avenues that blogging may take you. But remember to be open to these changes and opportunities that come your way. Don't be so tied to one idea that it prevents you from other growth for you and your blog.

The other piece of information I want to leave you with is to make sure you treat your blog like a business. You must always remember to write regularly. Not just when you feel like it. Post to your social media profiles when you publish new content.

With your credibility established you can become a speaker, run workshops, charge ridiculous prices for consulting or go after any number of lucrative business opportunities. The key is to build the foundation to leverage from, and you have no excuses now since you have been given the tools to do this with your blog.

Blogger Interviews

Keren Brown – Author, Food Lovers' Guide to
Seattle, Blogger at Frantic Foodie

1. How did you get started with writing about
food and drinks?

I moved to Seattle and didn't know a soul and I
started baking and cooking out of boredom.
Then I found an online newspaper that I could
blog about food and it all started.

2. What's your favorite type of food?

Middle Eastern food. I love it. And I love Mexican. Especially home-made tortillas.

3. Where is your go to spot in your city where you know you can always have a great meal, whatever it may be?

My go to spot in Seattle is Poppy. It is a casual dining restaurant that serves Northwest food with an Indian flare. The food is served in Thalis, little platters with all different foods. They use beautiful spices that complement the best ingredients with a focus on vegetables. I especially love the dessert Thali, a really nice tasting menu of desserts.

4. Tell us a little about what your career involves. The idea here is to show bloggers that writing / blogging can take you in many directions and that there isn't one clear path.

My career involves many things. I write, eat out a lot, blog about it. I also have an event business called Foodportunity. Foodportunity is a line of networking events that connect the food community. I also work with food related startups. I help them connect with the food world and understand how it works. I love working with entrepreneurs because ideas are always brewing.

5. What is something you wish you knew before you started blogging? Or something you wish you learned early on?

I learned early on that every time you meet someone, that is a new connection. You need to add people to your social networks, even if you don't intend to start a business out of it. Sometimes people you don't expect can become really close friends and you end up working with someone later. Establish relationships early with anyone who comments on your blog.

6. Tell us what your 3 favorite tools or online resources are.

1) Facebook Groups (for meeting people and getting and giving advice)

2) Card Munch from Linkedin to make connections. You scan business cards with it and it immediately sends an invite to linked in.

3) Audible, an app that lets you listen to books. I sometimes listen while I am working on my blog photos, or uploading stuff.

7. What do you do to stay fit?

I run after my 3 kids under 4. I also try to do Pilates or Yoga.

8. Do you have any advice for aspiring bloggers?

Try not to compare yourself to other bloggers. If you start off comparing then it might intimidate you. Don't expect your blog from the beginning to have the best writing, best photography and best everything. Just focus on writing and getting it out. Your voice is what counts, and with time, you will find it. If you don't start somewhere, you may never get anywhere.

9. Who is your hero?

Martha Stewart. I just admire everything that she has achieved.

10. Anything else that you want to add?

Keep it real. Don't get caught up in popularity contests. Make sure you do what you believe and your passion for the subject will attract others.

Sucheta Rawal – Founder, Non-profit, GO Eat Give

1. How did you get started with writing about food and drinks?

I was always a big foodie and loved to cook and entertain. My friends would call me for restaurant advice and cooking tips. One of them introduced me to a friend who was the editor of a South Asian magazine based in Atlanta. So I approached them and started writing their section on restaurant reviews. That's where the food writing started!

2. What's your favorite type of food?

I love anything made with fresh ingredients where you can taste real food (not the modified unrecognized version of it). Also, I like to experiment with a lot of different kinds of spices. Having said that, my two favorite cuisines are Italian and Indian.

3. Where is your go to spot in your city where you know you can always have a great meal, whatever it may be?

Right now, my go to spot is Chai Pani in Decatur. They serve Indian street food and the specials change daily. I go there almost every week & have never been disappointed :)
4. Tell us a little about what your career involves. (The idea here to show bloggers that writing / blogging can take you in many directions and that there isn't one clear path.)

When I started doing restaurant reviews, it was purely as a hobby while I held a full time corporate job to pay bills. I started contributing to more magazines, teaching cooking classes, and finally incorporated a lot of travel writing. If there is one thing I enjoy more than food, it is traveling! As more friends encouraged me to share my unique voice on exploring countries, I created a blog called "Go Eat Give." Here I wrote about restaurants, recipes, travel destinations, volunteer programs and culture. As the popularity of the blog grew, I started getting invited for speaking engagements and interviews.

Now, Go Eat Give is officially a 501c3 nonprofit organization. We have expanded our services from a FREE blog covering 40+ countries, to international cooking classes, monthly cultural awareness Destination events & volunteer vacation programs around the world. We work with partner nonprofits in Cuba, India, Indonesia, Nepal, Spain, Kenya & South Africa.

I don't spend as much time blogging now, since I lead some of these tours & coordinatie the Destination dinners, but it has been very exciting to see how the concept has impacted lives of people locally and globally. When I started my blog, I had no idea it would blossom to be what it is today!

5. What is something you wish you knew before you started blogging? Or something you wish you learned early on?

One of the things I wished someone had told me before I started blogging is - have an intention for your blog and every blog post you write. Sure, you want to share opinions and keep your own voice, but when you are broadcasting to the world wide web, it stays out there forever! Readers create a perception of you and your writing. If you want to write a journal, you can keep your posts on "private" setting, but if you want to be known as a credible writer, make sure your every post is well thought out, meaningful and free of grammatical errors.

Another fact I learned from experience is that it is very time consuming to do exactly that: write a well constructed 500-800 words blog post, with properly formatted photos, linking back to websites and sharing it on social media. It takes me average of 2-3 hours to complete a blog from start to finish. So if you are thinking updating your blog is something you plan to do after you finish cooking dinner and tuck the kids into bed, make sure you have allotted enough time for yourself.

6. Tell us what your 3 favorite tools or online resources are.

Wikipedia: I always check facts before posting my articles.
Pinterest and Google images: Good for inspiration especially when I want to experiment with a new dish.

7. What do you do to stay fit?

I always start my day with a light meal (tea, fruit, eggs) so that I don't have to deprive myself of anything for the rest of the day. When I'm not traveling, I try to cook healthy at home as much as I can, eating mostly vegetarian.

Yoga keeps me aligned physically and mentally when I'm traveling. It also helps with digestion (after those big meals) and back pains (resulting from long flights).

8. Do you have any advice for aspiring bloggers?

I started my blog just as a means to share my passion for food and travel, but I think often times new bloggers think their blog would be their business. Selling ads and getting free meals is great. However, if you want to quit your job and follow your passion, it has to involve selling other skills that companies are actually willing to pay for.

Another common mistake I see with many bloggers is that when they start blogging, they are very enthusiastic about it, but after a few months you begin to see fewer and fewer posts, and eventually the blog becomes a grave site of some delicious reviews. While its discouraging to not see your Google Analytics skyrocket after you posted the recipe of your most raved about cheesecake, you must not lose hope and you do have to keep at it. Consistency and persistence are keys to running a successful blog. It takes a long time and a lot of hard work to build strong traffic.

9. Who is your hero?

My formative years were most influenced by my grandmother in India, whom I grew up with. She would host travelers from around the world, and spoil them with her delicious food and generous hospitality. I also used to accompany her to do charity work and participate in cultural events in our hometown. She was perhaps the most socially active lady in town, and still is at 80+ years!

10. What has been your biggest accomplishment?

The powerful impact of "Go Eat Give" makes me feel very accomplished. After every "destination dinner" or a volunteer trip, I see the reaction of the people who have participated. Some of them are deeply influenced by the culture and take back some learning that they had never imagined. Practically everyone who has been on a trip with me has had a life-altering moment. Also, when I see our attendees break into a group dance (be it Afghan or Bollywood) & have a fun time, I feel great about being able to create that positive experience for them.

Winning the "top 5 most influential cultural bloggers in the world" in 2012 was also a nice pat on the back.

Being a Blogger: Dennis Byron aka Ale Sharpton, Beer Blogger, Speaker and Event Host

1. How did you get started with writing about food and drinks?

When attending Cornell University, I took it for granted that I did so well in my writing and communications courses. It wasn't until I finished my college career when I actually considered making journalism an actual profession. Since I have a long line of chefs and caterers in my family—we're talking generations—I embraced that with my passion for exploring the world of beer. To add, Atlanta is such a great city for this, so it was a no-brainer to make that my focus.

2. What's your favorite type of food?

I went with the simple formula: If there is a food I couldn't do without, what would it be? Hence, I came to the realization that I am a seafood fanatic. Specifically, baked or broiled salmon and crab (specifically legs and cakes). If beer was considered a food source, that would be first.

3. Where is your go to spot in your city where you know you can always have a great meal, whatever it may be?

Having a great meal in Atlanta is pretty easy to do, but having it balanced with a great beer selection is another story. So with that being considered, you can't lose with Cook Hall, Georgia Pine, or JCT Kitchen for starters. I'm a Libra, so I am a bit indecisive. Sorry!

4. Tell us a little about what your career involves. The idea here to show bloggers that writing and blogging can take you in many directions and that there isn't one clear path.

I thrive on informing my readers that there is more to beer than ratings and criticism. I cherish writing in my own voice what I consider great beers, breweries, gastro pubs, restaurants, attractions, hotels and most importantly people to meet in any city I visit both nationally and abroad. With this framework, it's virtually unlimited what I can write about.

5. What is something you wish you knew before you started blogging? Or something you wish you learned early on?

Truly, nothing comes to mind. Blogging is an ongoing learning experience and I cherish every minute. If anything, I wish I had started earlier. It's a fun challenge to build your identity as a blogger and candidly share your experience while broadening your audience.

6. Tell us what your 3 favorite tools or online resources are.

One, I enjoy tweeting because it's my way of doing what easily could be a blog post in a limited amount of characters. Two, I love having the ability to research any beer through various reliable platforms including BeerAdvocate.com, RateBeer.com, BeerSTreetJournal.com, and BeerPulse.com. And three, in general, I love Google.

7. What do you do to stay fit?

I do 100 push-ups and 100 sit ups daily, run two miles every three days, eat small portions, no desserts, no soda, no breakfast, and only taste beef and pork. Oh, and three servings of quality beer. We can call that the Ale Sharpton diet. (DVDs are available.)

8. Do you have any advice for aspiring bloggers?

Do not be afraid of expressing your voice, but just do so tastefully...and factually. Also, do your best to know AP standards. This is a great framework to help structure your writing and keep things in check. People will be turned off by too many grammatical errors and unnecessary rambling. Last, know the difference between writing for magazines and Web writing. They are totally different fields. Oh yeah, besides having a Twitter account, being a great photographer surely helps too. Evidently, with all of these new apps, people like pictures!

9. Who is your hero?

My mother, Brenda. She was fearless, spoke her mind, loved teaching and was simply a downright genius. She made me what I am today. I miss her crazily.

10. What do you love most about blogging?

The ability to meet people, set your own deadlines, be your own boss, speak your voice, and explore the world due to the power of the pen—err...keyboard. Having a camera in tow to document your experiences and posting your shots later is also very rewarding.

Bonus Traffic Getters

Create an index in Wikipedia for you and your blog. It won't get a lot of traffic, but it is good to have it there.

Put your blog link and relevant social media profiles on your email signature. You can create a professional looking signature at wisestamp for free.

Create a survey. If you've got some decent traffic create a survey and publish the results. If you want to get really creative, make an infographic. People love these and they spread like wildfire.

Give away adspace. If you have empty slots for ads, why not give one away to a charity in your area? Promote that you will be doing it on your blog in a post and then ask people to nominate their favorite charity.

Create a Squidoo lens for your blog. Again this may not be a huge traffic generator but squidoo is an authority site, so good for getting some inbound links.

Made in the USA
Lexington, KY
12 May 2015